PROTECTING
OUR MOST
VALUABLE TREASURES
IN OUR
CHURCHES
AND
SCHOOLS
AND ELSEWHERE

BY DARRIN LEE PRUETT

WESTBOW
PRESS®
A DIVISION OF THOMAS NELSON
& ZONDERVAN

WestBow Press books may be ordered through booksellers or by contacting:

WestBow Press
A Division of Thomas Nelson & Zondervan
1663 Liberty Drive
Bloomington, IN 47403
www.westbowpress.com
1 (866) 928-1240

ISBN: 978-1-9736-9024-5 (sc)
ISBN: 978-1-9736-9025-2 (hc)
ISBN: 978-1-9736-9023-8 (e)

Library of Congress Control Number: 2020906959

Print information available on the last page.

WestBow Press rev. date: 04/30/2020

CONTENTS

WHAT COULD I DO?

I N RECENT HISTORY, brothers and sisters in Christ have been killed during worship services or in other tragic instances; Christians have been killed just for being Christian. There also have been senseless killings in our schools, streets, and other public areas. I have been deeply saddened and hurt by these tragic events.

I prayed about it and asked the Lord, "Is there anything I can do?" The answer that came to my heart was to be prayerful, diligent, and watchful in my own life and to teach my family to be prayerful, diligent, and watchful.

I also felt strongly in my heart that I should write this book, with the hope that churches will develop a security and safety plan, that schools will take measures to keep our children safe if, and that we, as individuals, will train ourselves to be *alert* and *aware* of our surroundings and be prepared to react appropriately if we are exposed to danger or an emergency situation.

As with all things, pray about it to our Father in heaven in the name of His Son, our Lord and Savior Jesus Christ, and let the Holy Spirit guide you.

INTRODUCTION
PARADIGM SHIFT

Y EARS AGO, I was newly hired as an oil refinery operator and was put through an extensive training class, during which a video was shown about paradigm shift. The video was intended to inspire and encourage us new oil refinery operators to speak up if we saw a better way of doing things; to introduce new ideas, instead of accepting the status quo just because it was the way things had been done. It was the first time I'd heard the term *paradigm shift*, and I thought what it was. Was it taking two dimes from one pocket and shifting them to another pocket?

I learned the definition of *paradigm* is "a typical example or pattern, a model," and a *paradigm shift* refers to changing the typical pattern.

The paradigm in so many churches and schools has been to hold worship services or Bible studies without considering any security measures and to send our children to school, taking only minimum security measures and just assuming everything will be fine.

I have been in the church all my life, and in my experience, I have rarely, if ever, heard a discussion on safety and security—that is, until recently. I believe that this paradigm is changing. In fact, while preparing for this book, I asked various preachers, ministers, and church leaders if they had a security plan for the congregation, and they confirmed that they do.

For those in the church who think a security plan is not needed, consider this: is there a security plan for the collection? In general, at least two people will take the collection money to a secured room. The money will be locked up, and later, someone will deposit that money in the bank. When that money is in the bank, it will be guarded and protected.

What about our personal money? When we put our money in the bank, we expect the bank to have security measures, including armed guards, to keep our money safe. If the bank didn't have security measures, we would not patronize that bank.

So we consider the security for the collection money and our personal money, but aren't our lives and especially the lives of our children more precious than our money?

In the title of this book, *Protecting Our Most Valuable Treasures in Our Churches and Schools*, I believe it is clear what is meant by "our most valuable treasures." When a friend asked me when I was going to write my next book I told him that I was working on a book with this title, he asked, "Why don't you just call it *Protecting Our Children*?"—he understood right away what I meant by the title.

"Exactly!" I said, "What is more valuable than our children?"

We may have certain expectations for our money's security but not have the same expectations for our personal security.

Suppose there is a church where the leadership says something like, "No firearms allowed. We are going to leave it to the Lord to protect us." Would they say the same thing about the collection money or their personal funds, such as, "No firearms allowed in the bank. We will leave it to the Lord to protect our money"?

CHAPTER 1
COMMUNICATION AND PREVENTIVE STEPS

O NE SUNDAY A few years ago, while preaching in the small congregation where I worshipped, I wanted to emphasize the importance of our staying faithful to Jesus Christ unto death. I asked the congregation to imagine that armed men came into the building and overpowered everyone and then these men go to each of us, one by one, and told us to deny Jesus Christ; whoever didn't deny Jesus Christ would be killed immediately.

After worship services, a sister told me that I had scared the children by creating that scenario. When I prepared that sermon, I remembered hearing a similar sermon as a child. The preacher had talked about being faithful unto death, except he brought up the early history of the church when Christians were persecuted. Nowadays, if you offer examples of Christians being killed if they don't deny Christ, you don't have to recall the early history of the church; you can bring up current events.

The persecution of Christians is nothing new, even here in the United States. All my life, I've heard about the beautiful young ladies who were killed by a bomb planted under the steps of a church in Birmingham, Alabama. A few years ago in Egypt, Christians were taken off a bus by a group of terrorists and told to deny Christ; when they didn't deny Christ, they were shot and killed.

I have a friend from Ghana who is currently in Egypt, spreading the Word. God be with them.

Of course, as Christians, we are to remain faithful to Christ unto death, but that doesn't mean we are not to have security and safety measures.

In the Bible, the word *pastor* is interchangeable with the word *shepherd*. During biblical times, the shepherds who tended to the flocks were not necessarily the owners of the sheep. That is the relationship that pastors have with the church—the church is the Lord's church and the pastors are shepherds for the

Lord's flock. Of course, that is for spiritual matters, but like the shepherds who watched over the sheep, that includes watching over the safety of the church.

Some might say that they will just pray about it and trust God to protect us. I want to point out that God is all-powerful and God's Will, will be done, but consider this: when Moses and the Israelites were crossing the wilderness, God's angel went before them and protected them. God parted the sea and brought it back down upon the Egyptians after the Israelites had crossed to the other side. But did God say, "Y'all just walk on through the desert, and I will take care of you"? God did take care of them on their journey, but He did not have them walk through the desert, carefree.

God had Moses number the men over a certain age and made into armies, and God told Moses at which position each of the armies would set out and march through the desert. Even though God did take care of them, and God's angel was right there to smack down any enemies, God still had the Israelites prepare.

Of course, we should pray about it but also be diligent, vigilant, watchful, and prepared. It does not negate faith in God to be prepared and have a security plan. It is very important to have regular discussions about safety and security and to have a plan. Each time there is a meeting about the business of the church, the subject of safety and security should be included.

Communicate with Neighbors and Police

Not only should there be communication within the church but also with the surrounding community, such as law enforcement and neighbors.

Unless you are in a country where the police are among the church's oppressors, such as where being a Christian is against the law, then meet with the local police. Ask police and other emergency personnel—firefighters and ambulances—how long, in general, it will take to respond to your location if called for an emergency. This is important to know. For example, police may come from a different area than fire or ambulance emergency services. You could be located where emergency personnel are right around the corner, or they could be miles away.

Communicate with the neighbors and businesses near the church building. Ask the neighbors to keep their eyes open, and give them have a contact number for the church.

Find out which church members live nearby and who drives by regularly, and ask them to keep an eye out for anything out of the ordinary. Some churches have someone on the premises each day, such as groundskeepers or office workers, but some churches don't have anyone in the building or on their property except at meetings or to clean up. .

Security System

If possible, install a security system in the church building. A wide range of security systems are available, from a basic system to more advanced systems. A basic security system will alert the designated person and/or the police if the alarm is triggered. A more advanced system will include cameras that can be monitored remotely. Security guards could be hired to watch the church building, or members of the church could take turns watching the building, depending on the budget and the church's needs.

If the property isn't fenced, consider installing a fence, and keep the gate locked. If all church members desire access to the church at all times, put a combination lock on the gate, and give the church members the combination and a key to the building, or use door locks that require a combination.

Make sure all crawl spaces and attic spaces are locked and secured, especially those with entrances from outside.

Come Early and Take a Look Around

Before worship services, Bible study, events, or meetings, someone should come an hour or two early and do a thorough walk-through of the property, looking for anything suspicious or dangerous— anything out of place, persons in hiding, or things that don't belong. An explosive device wouldn't necessarily be so obvious as to have sticks of dynamite with wires and a timer; it may be inconspicuous, for example in a bag or backpack.

Use and develop your instincts when you look around. Watch for things that are obvious but also for things out of place and perhaps not so obvious. Check the open spaces, but also check closets and bathrooms.

During the walk-through, keep an eye out for other dangerous things, such as wasp nests, snakes, spiders (such as black widows), or poison ivy along the edge of the building or on the property.

If possible, have two or more people do thorough walk-throughs. If two or more aren't available, at least one person should do a walk-through before the congregation arrives.

- Communicate, discuss, and develop a security and safety plan.
- Communicate with neighbors and emergency services.
- Monitor the meeting place to ensure there are no harmful objects or devices.
- Consider installing a fence and/or alarm or monitoring system.
- Make a thorough walk-through of the property before worship services or a meeting.
- Secure crawl space entrances.

CHAPTER 2
BE DILIGENT, BE PREPARED

OUR LOCAL PREACHER has a talent for putting things into words, and he recently spoke about some of the tragic events of violence. He said, "While the main focus of the church is the Word and serving God and doing God's will, which we will do, the Holy Spirit has imparted to the elders to make a contingency plan for the possibility of an attacker. While I won't go into the details of the security plan, I can say that basically, if something happens, such as gun shots, then get yourself to safety. If the Holy Spirit imparts to you that you can stop the attacker, and you believe you can do so without getting in the way of someone else who is trying to stop the attacker, then do so."

As an example, suppose someone comes in with a

firearm and starts shooting or is about to shoot. I have a walking stick, and I think I can whop him on the head with it, but then I see another brother or sister who has a gun and therefore is better equipped to stop the intruder. I need to make sure I don't get in the way of the brother or sister with a gun.

Front and Center

Years ago, a coworker invited me to his wedding, which was to take place after worship in the church building. I arrived a bit early, and worship services were still taking place. When I arrived, I noticed a group of men standing in front of the entrance to the church building. As I parked my motorcycle and walked toward the building, I noticed that this small group of men had their eyes on me. They were wearing suits, whereas I had on steel-toed boots and a leather jacket, so I can see how I stood out some.

As I got closer, one young man said gruffly, "Can I help you?"

"I was invited to a wedding," I said, and I mentioned my coworker's name.

Then he directed me inside.

While I didn't feel welcomed by this man's

demeanor or tone of voice, I did understand, and I liked the idea of someone being there at the entrance to watch.

My coworker later explained that it was their practice to have someone at the front door entrance as a security measure and to greet people when they arrived.

Someone stationed at the entrance, welcoming people and holding the door open, makes people feel welcome and, at the same time, is a good security measure. The greeter at the door can be trained in what to do if danger approaches. For instance, suppose someone approaches with a gun, machete, knife, or other weapon. The greeter could immediately step inside, lock the door, and call out an alarm.

Suppose a stranger comes to the building, acting nervous or displaying other odd behavior. In a caring and courteous way, the greeter can ask about the person's welfare—such as saying, "Are you okay?"— and then listen intently to what and how the person answers. Church members could take training to determine other signs to look out for that could indicate someone is out to do harm.

It's good to have at least two people as greeters at the

door. While one is welcoming and doing most of the speaking to the people, the other can be watching and be ready to sound an alarm, if necessary, or perhaps get an elder, deacon, minister, or someone with a more training, if need be.

The greeters need to be trained in security measures, but it's also very important to know how to greet people in a warm and caring way so that people are welcomed with love.

Station a greeter at each unlocked entrance. All entrances without a greeter should be locked on the outside so no one can enter, but they should be able to open from the inside to get out in case of an emergency. An alarm should be installed, if practical, that will sound if the door is opened.

Smaller church buildings might use only one entrance, while larger church buildings may use multiple entrances, but these entrances must be manned, and there should be alarms on the entrances that are not in use and manned.

Do not allow backpacks in the church building, and watch for people wearing bulky clothing, such as big coats, that may look out of place.

In addition to the greeters, there can be individuals

or teams to patrol and do walk-arounds inside and around the outside of the building—whatever need is determined, based on the size of the building.

Arming Security Teams

Should the security teams be armed with firearms? I think so. For those who don't agree, consider the collection money and church funds. When it's put in the bank, we expect the money to be protected by armed guards.

I've heard of congregations whose local leadership strictly forbids anyone coming in with a firearm on the other hand, I heard of a church where the members were encouraged to carry firearms. I also heard of a church in Colorado Springs, Colorado, where a shooter was shot and stopped by a member of an armed security team.

Think about countries where guns aren't present. When evil people go about to do harm, they either have guns, even if it's against the law, or they use something else, such as machetes, knives, or improvised explosive devices. When evil people want to do harm to others, they find a way.

Training

It is most important that individuals are trained in the use and safety of the weapons they have. If members of a security team are armed with guns, then they need to be trained in the safety and use of the gun. If someone has a walking stick, he or she needs to learn how to use the walking stick for protection and self-defense. Whether someone attacks the church with a firearm, machete, or other weapon, that person needs to be stopped.

Be knowledgeable of the laws in your area regarding the carrying of firearms. Some states are open-carry, and some states require a license.

Train Sunday school teachers and nursery attendants in how to keep the children safe. First, determine the best location for the nursery or cry room. I'd suggest putting the nursery in an out-of-the-way room, if possible, instead of being the first door when entering the building. Train the attendants or teachers to immediately lock the door if an alarm is sounded.

Train the church members on what to do in an emergency and to always be aware of their surroundings. At the very least, train a security/safety team, but you might have drills for the congregation and go over escape routes and danger warning signals. You might ask the church to come out on a Saturday to have a couple of drills and singing.

Everyone should be aware of their surroundings and the escape routes or attack plan. I usually sit in the back, where I'm close to the entrance. That way, I can see and hear when someone enters.

In a small congregation where I once was a deacon, instead of sitting in the pews, I would stand or sit by the entrance. I would watch the entrance and greet people when they came in. I checked the parking lot entrance regularly. If services let out at night, my son or I would escort unaccompanied ladies to their cars.

If the Holy Spirit puts it in you to serve in such a way, then listen.

In addition to the greeters, which is the first line of defense, strategically place security team members. Place a few chairs next to the entrance against the wall. Church buildings have different layouts, so discuss your best options and make a plan.

Survey Members' Talents

Ask people what they can do. Do a survey of the members to determine who is military or former military, police, martial arts instructors or students, self-defense instructors, firearms instructors, or hunters. Ask for volunteers for security and safety teams and instructors. If no one in the congregation can lead in-house training, then seek training elsewhere. Encourage the church members to take martial arts courses, self-defense classes, and weapons/firearms training.

I had a martial arts instructor who, at the close of class, would say things like, "Watch your back"; "Don't hurt anyone that ain't hurting you"; or "Pray for peace, and train for war." Being trained and vigilant and having a security and safety plan is not living in fear; it's being prepared. Hopefully, you won't have to use your training, but like auto insurance, you want to have it if you need it.

Prepare yourself and train. Run drills of different scenarios. For example, have fire drills. Have a drill for what to do if a person comes in to do harm. Develop and use your instincts.

In addition to defense training, train in first aid and CPR. Do a survey of the members to determine who are nurses, doctors, emergency medical technicians, or firefighters.

Thou Shalt Not Kill

The Lord's commandment of thou shall not kill is for murder, or thou shall not murder. Remember, though, if someone is hurting or trying to hurt you, your family, or the congregation, our purpose is to stop that person. The best way to stop that person is by using *deadly force*, which is force that is likely to cause serious bodily harm or death. We are to use deadly force only when our lives and the lives of others are threatened.

Now, suppose an attacker is stopped by deadly force. He hasn't died but is seriously injured, and you are certain that he is no longer a threat. Do you then shoot him in the head? No. You should call the police, but also get the attacker an ambulance.

Our purpose is not to kill attackers but to stop them, and the best way to stop them is to apply deadly force. So, the purpose is stopping the attacker, the death of the attacker may be the outcome.

Stopping the Attacker

If an intruder tries to hurt you and your loved ones, you should get yourself and your loved ones to safety, if possible. However, if you attempt to stop the intruder, do not be nicey-nicey and just wound the person or shoot him in the leg. Your goal is to stop him. The best way to stop someone is to apply seriously strong force—deadly force.

As previously mentioned, deadly force is an action taken on an individual or individuals that can cause great bodily injury or death. For example, if you have a gun, the best way to stop someone who is trying to cause harm is to shoot that person in the largest part of the body—the chest or midsection—where it will do the most damage. If you only have a club, the best way to stop the person is to whack the club as hard as you can on his head or wherever you can reach.

If you hesitate, thinking you can't kill someone, realize that the person is trying to kill you or your loved ones, and you are stopping that. If the attacker dies, then he dies, but that shouldn't be your purpose; your purpose is to stop him.

As I've said, if the attacker is gravely wounded and subdued and is no threat whatsoever, don't shoot him in the head to make sure he's dead. Call the emergency personnel—police and an ambulance.

- Place greeters at the entrances—two at each entrance, if possible.
- Lock other entrances from the outside.
- Develop and train security teams.
- Pray for peace and safety, but be trained and prepared for emergencies or an attack.

CHAPTER 3
PROTECTING OUR CHILDREN IN SCHOOLS

My HEART QUAKES from knowing about tragic events, where evil persons have gone into schools and killed innocent children. I have children, and I can't imagine the hurt and sadness of parents who have lost children to such tragedies.

Our Children Are Not Political Pawns

I hear a lot of people say, "We have to do something," but for just about everything that is proposed, someone has a reason not to do it.

"Hire armed guards. Secure the schools." Then someone says, "I don't want my child's school to be like a prison," or "I don't want guns anywhere near my children."

For those who don't want their children protected by trained personnel with firearms, do they avoid taking their children into a bank, amusement park, or even grocery stores where there are armed guards?

When it comes to our children's safety, why is there such opposition to safety measures and preventive steps that are put in place or suggested?

As a society, we figured out how to secure our gold, money, jewelry, and other treasures. When you go into a bank or jewelry store, look around. You may see armed guards, and there may be only one way in and out. Safety measures are in place to keep the valuables safe.

Years ago, there was a shooting in a Riverside, California, courthouse. Since that time, anyone entering a courthouse in California must pass through a metal detector.

Immediately after the evil mass murders of September 11, 2001, where hijackers took over airliners and ran them into the World Trade Center and the Pentagon, preventive steps were taken to ensure safety on the airliners and in the airports, which included a thick and secure door to the cockpit to prevent anyone from entering, increased security to get into the boarding areas, and an increased number of air marshals. Real safety solutions were enacted.

There was a tragic shooting at the Inland Regional Center in San Bernardino. I recently went there to do some business regarding my son, Jcori. A guard stood outside the front door, which was locked, to screen people before they are allowed into the building.

As a society, we are good at protecting our money and other treasures, and sometimes when there are killings, safety measures are put in place quickly. Why, then, is there so much resistance when it is about our children in school?

Some say they don't want guns, guards, or metal detectors in the schools, but does that apply to amusement parks? The last time I went to an amusement park there were guns, guards, and metal detectors.

Consider this: these cowards go where the most vulnerable are. We leave our schools vulnerable, but where are we more vulnerable than in hospitals? Yet if you go to a hospital, there are armed guards at the entrance. You have to sign in. There are certain areas where only authorized people can go, and the doors are kept locked; authorized personnel have badges that open the doors.

Tall Fences

We need to make our schools secure. If there is not a tall fence around the school, then one should be installed. Survey where there are weak areas. Have one entry point to get onto school grounds during school hours, and limit the entrances when students are arriving or leaving.

Some people argue that putting a fence around a school will make the school look like a prison. That is because the paradigm is that prisons are secure, and schools are not secure. Someone might say that putting a fence around a school makes it look like a military base, or the United States Mint, or a power plant, or a refinery, or anywhere else that we view as a secure place. We need to reach a point where we think that a fence around a school makes it look like a secure school.

If your child's school or a school in your area doesn't have a fence, demand that a fence be installed. A school should be fenced and have only one entry point (or limited entry points) onto the school property that is monitored at all times.

Secure School Entrances

At one school that some of my children attend, although a visitor has to sign in and get buzzed in, the fence around the school is only waist-high. Someone could easily jump over the waist-high fence.

I suggest using strong and secure doors. During school hours, people should need badges, like they have in hospitals, to open doors to the part of the school where the children are. Do not allow anyone in unless necessary. Have visitors sign in and present identification.

When a visitor comes to see a teacher or student, he or she should wait in the front office. If the visitor is for a teacher, he or she will have to wait until the teacher take get a break. Of course, parents may want to see the classroom from time to time, but they should be checked in and escorted to the room.

Install alert buttons. Consider a bank: if someone comes in to rob a bank, bank workers can push buttons that will alert the police. Install such buttons in schools; when the buttons are pressed, the police will be alerted, and alerts also will go out to teachers to secure the classroom and lock the doors.

During the busy hours, such as the arriving and leaving times, ask the police to be present in front of the school. Increase the guards and faculty present in front of and around the outside areas or hallways of the school.

Guards

If we lived in a world where the only weapons were swords, spears, and machetes, then we would have strong men as guards, with swords, spears, and machetes, to protect our children. If we lived in a world where rocks were the only weapon, then we would have guards with rocks. I think the schools should have trained armed guards.

I was listening to a radio talk show in which the radio show participants were discussing whether schools should have armed guards. One woman whined loudly, "I don't want my world to be like that—where there are armed guards in schools." However, I doubt she had a problem living in a world where money in a bank and jewelry in a jewelry store are guarded by armed guards. When it's about banks or jewelry stores and other such "treasures," having armed guards is never discussed. What kind of world is it where money and jewelry get more protection than our children; and where it's a problem if someone mentions protecting children with armed guards? Our children are much more precious than all the money or jewels in the world.

Our minds have been conditioned to having armed guards for our money or jewelry—in fact, it's expected—but having armed guards for our children is a problem for some people.

When my two oldest children were in elementary school, at least two of their teachers were military veterans. I'm sure both of these strong women had been trained in the use of firearms. I think that teachers who are qualified and are willing should be allowed to have firearms. Now, I'm not saying that all teachers should carry pistols, but a small safe could keep firearms secure and allow them to be accessed quickly.

It is a paradigm that our jewelry stores, banks, and even pawn shops have armed guards to protect the jewelry, money, and merchandise, but if we consider having armed guards to protect our children, some say they don't want to live in a world like that.

Still, we live in a world where everybody isn't nice, and we accept armed guards to protect our valuables— our "treasures." Shouldn't we treasure our children more? I think there needs to be a paradigm shift with this way of thinking.

I heard another radio show participant comment on armed guards or armed faculty at his daughter's school. He said he didn't want firearms near his daughter. I wondered if he avoided taking his daughter into banks or jewelry stores. We want our money and valuables to be protected, but aren't our children more valuable than our possessions?

I heard someone on the news say that we don't need guards or faculty to be armed in schools because if a shooter enters the building, we don't need a gunfight, with bullets going in all directions. Why, then, don't we say that we don't need bank guards to have guns because we don't want customers and bank employees to be in danger of a gunfight. Again, why are our money and treasures a higher priority than our children?

Why does this society value money and jewelry

over our children? Why is it okay that politicians and the wealthy have armed security guards, but it's a problem when we suggest guards for our children?

Why have we gotten so far away from our basic instincts of protecting our children? Animals have basic instincts to protect their young. All hunters know that if they come across a bear and cubs, they shouldn't get between the mother and the cubs. Anyone raised on a farm probably has been flogged by a hen protecting her eggs. But when it comes to protecting our children, there is always resistance and excuses. When there have been tragic events, where an evil person has come to a school and killed children, why do people talk about legislation for gun control, instead of discussing how to make schools safer?

If a colony of bees swarmed onto a school campus and stung the children, we wouldn't talk about legislating beekeepers. We would get the bees off the campus and work to keep them off campus.

When there is a school shooting, why is there talk about banning assault rifles and automatic rifles? Automatic rifles are already banned. Automatic rifles are rifles that have rapid fire; if you keep your finger on the trigger, it continues to fire.

What is an "assault rifle"? If someone attacks someone else with a pencil, doesn't that become an assault pencil? Then all pencils have the potential to become assault pencils. So if someone wants to ban "assault pencils," then they are talking about banning all pencils.

I grew up around firearms and knives. The long guns I grew up with had wooden stocks. The same rifles or shotguns are also made with black plastic with finger grooves. Our minds tell us that that the black plastic stocks are scarier, but they are the same firearms as those with wooden stocks. The look and composition of the stocks does not change the capabilities of the firearm.

The same goes for knives. I grew up with hunting knives, such as Bowie knives, but when I was in the Marines, the knives were black steel with black handles. Yet you have the same capabilities with one knife as you do with the other. If a government wanted to ban one type of knife, then they would want to ban the other type of knife.

The people who want to take guns away from law-abiding citizens should take their money out of banks, where there are armed guards, and demand that no one ever protect them or their money with a firearm.

Why are people so quick to give up their right of self-protection? When there is a shooting in school or anywhere, and people jump and start talking about gun control, they aren't calling for safety in our schools; they are calling for everyone else to be as vulnerable as they want to leave children vulnerable at school. Why would people want us to be vulnerable?

What? No Door Locks on Classroom Doors?

Some schools don't have locks on the classroom doors. Why wouldn't there be locks on the classroom doors?

Some classrooms do not have an outside door; the only classroom door opens to an inside hallway. Some of classrooms don't have locks on the doors. People have debated over whether to lock classrooms. You might think there would be security cameras in classrooms, but some argue that it would take away the teachers' privacy.

Banks and jewelry stores have security cameras. Bank workers and jewelers go about their work lives, knowing there is always a camera on them. Again, when it's a matter of protecting our treasured possessions, security cameras are not questioned. Don't we value our children more?

Let's compare classrooms that open into a hallway with classrooms that open to the outside. With classrooms that have an outside door, it is never questioned that the door must have a lock. This prevents theft or vandalism when school is not in session. Remember that children are more precious than property, yet it seems that protecting the material things inside the classroom and school isn't questioned, but protecting our children is.

Classrooms with doors that open into a hallway also should have locks on the doors, which can be unlocked from the inside without a key and from the outside with a key.

Teachers should have a key to their classrooms. Principals, vice principals, and select staff should have master keys. Those who have master keys should be people who would not give up that key, even if it meant their lives or the life of the perpetrator.

Security devices are available that secure the doors at the bottom, which prevents the doors from opening. The door would have to be broken for anyone to come in. Of course, that would depend on the strength of the door.

When Schools Say "We Don't Have Money in the Budget for That."

Fences, locks, and other security features that help keep children safe should be at the top of a school's priorities.

What can parents do? Parents don't control the school's budget, but they can talk to the people in charge and demand that such things as fences, locks, and guards be implemented. Go to PTA meetings, school board meetings, or any other meetings at which parents can speak. Vote for candidates of public office who will put children's safety and security at the top of their agendas. Ask for details on how they will do that. Not those that talk about "gun control", but those that will make our schools secure and safe by implementing safety and security measures similar to banks and large amusement parks. Run for government positions so that you can implement safety and security measures in the schools.

Talk about Safety with Your Children

Have conversations with your children about what to do in certain situations. Have drills with them.

Teach your children what they should do if someone is shooting around the school? If you don't know what to do, go to the police station and ask them what a student should do in case of shooting at school. Ask your children if the school has safety and security related drills and ask them what they learned.

Teach your children to always be aware of their surroundings. Teach them to have a plan for what to do in emergency situations. Teach them that in emergency situations, they don't have to wait on an adult to tell them what to do. Of course, teaching a teen would be different from teaching a first-grader, but basically, if the danger is from an attacker, they should run and hide, and lock themselves in a room. If the danger is a fire, they should stay low and crawl out.

I heard on the radio recently that during a school shooting, a child hid inside a closet and locked the door. When the police came, they had to convince her that they truly were the police before she would unlock the door. I believe this child must have had good training.

Should students be allowed to have cell phones on them during school hours? I think so, but they should use them only in case of emergencies.

Vet School Employees

Find out how the teachers and other school employees are vetted. If there aren't background checks before hiring, demand that there should be. If a teacher or faculty member molests or hurts a child, that person must be reported, investigated by police, prosecuted, and fired, if it's true.

We teach our children to respect authority, but they need to know there are limits. Tell them not to undress for anyone or allow an adult to undress them. Tell them not to let anyone touch them on their private places. And remind them not to drink or eat anything that is not served in the cafeteria during a meal.

Student Threats

Students, if you hear threats of violence or see suspicious activity report it to the school authorities, parents, and police. Report it even if the threat or suspicious activity is from a friend. Even if you think the person making the threat is not serious report it.

Teachers and faculty let the students know that they can come to you and talk about problems and concerns. If a student is already comfortable talking to you they are more likely to come to you if they hear of danger.

Parents, talk often to your children about school. Ask them if they know of any danger and let them know to immediately report it to the school if they know of any danger. Also find out from the school what their policy is of handling threats from students.

Too Much Talk about the Perpetrators

When a shooting takes place in a church, school, theater, college, or wherever, I think far too much attention and discussion is given to the killer. The killer's name is repeated in the news over and over. The news reports go over the killer's life history, and people try to determine why the killer did it. When the next evil, deranged person comes along, he wants to get his name in the news also. I think that when an evil person commits such a heinous act, his (or her) name should never be mentioned, and if someone asks why the person did it, the answer simply should be, "Because he is evil."

The public, of course, wants information about the crime, but the news media takes it to far by constantly focusing on the perpetrator and even interviewing people who knew the killer. News reports seem to give these killers almost celebrity or hero status by constantly talking about them.

I suspect that not many of us could name one of our military men or women who was killed while serving our country or name someone serving in the military or as a firefighter police officer. But after an attack, the news people repeat the attacker's name over and over, and everybody learns and remembers the attacker's name.

When I first heard from my mother that my nephew, who was serving in the United States Army, was killed in action in Afghanistan, I was at the hospital, where my son, Jcori, had been admitted. Later, after composing myself and telling my children about their cousin's death, I turned on the TV in my son's hospital room, hoping to find out what had happened in Afghanistan. The only news I could find there was a small note at the bottom of the screen that mentioned that some servicemen were killed in Afghanistan— that was it. The "news" that the newscasters were actually talking about was something ridiculous that a young actress had done, which, to me, was just the diversion of the day.

Yet when someone kills innocent children or other innocent people, that killer's name is all over the news, which might be what the next sick, evil-minded person wants.

Stop Sensationalizing

Another sick practice by news media is to use tragedies for advertising. They sometimes take footage or sound bites of a previous tragedy and play that during their station, channel, or news program advertising. For example, I've heard announcements over the radio about various tragic events, and I think, *What? Again? That just happened the other day.* Then I realize it is an advertisement for the station's news department, using a previously covered event.

The news people are quick to put a label on these tragedies, such as "the largest mass shooting in the United States"—until there is one with more victims. Then they label that one the largest mass shooting in the United States.

Remember that the largest mass shooting in the United States was December 29, 1890, at Wounded

Knee, where an estimated three hundred Lakota were killed by US Cavalry troops. What were the Lakota doing? They were dancing and turning in their guns. For those who think everyone should turn in their guns to the government, think about the victims at Wounded Knee.

- Demand that our children be protected.
- Demand that schools have fences and one or more monitored entrances.
- Make sure classrooms can be locked.
- Be active in the PTA or other venues where parents can have a voice.
- Run for an office where you can make decisions about school safety.
- Ensure there is a vetting system for hiring new teachers and school employees.
- Listen to students, if they report threats and take action.

CHAPTER 4
WHILE OUT AND ABOUT

First, Back to the Basics

THERE HAS BEEN a paradigm shift in the way people conduct themselves in public, and it is not a good one. Instead of keeping their heads up and watching where they are walking, so many people walk with their heads down and their eyes on an electronic device in their hands. While walking in public places, such as a mall, I have had to dodge others who were walking while looking down at their phones.

I thought maybe I could invent an app where these people could put camera on their heads and a little window could show up on the corner of their phone screens, showing what's in front of them. Better than that, maybe these people could get back to the basics of walking and looking forward. The basics of walking with our heads up and watching where we are walking is important; to be aware of any impending danger, we must be aware of our surroundings.

Be Watchful and Diligent

Wherever you are, *always* be diligently aware of your surroundings Trust your instincts. Use your instincts. Develop your instincts. Always be watchful. Look around and take mental notes. Use your senses of sight, smell, and hearing, but use your sense of feeling too—like if you feel your hairs stand up, or your heart rate goes up, or you feel edgy or nervous or have an unusual alertness.

When walking in public, look at others; be aware of others. Speak a greeting. Look at people in the eye.

Instincts

Some people may not understand what instincts are. I consider instincts to be a feeling, intuition, or a sixth sense.

Animals have instincts. When I was a child, our family visited the zoo, where we saw a huge male gorilla in his habitat. There was a very thick glass wall between him and the crowd of people looking at him. The gorilla looked back at the crowd with a calm expression.

As my daddy and I approached the glass wall, the gorilla glared at us, and his expression became angry. Out of all the people there, he glared at my daddy; then he looked down at me and back up to my daddy. He glared at us for so long that the other people looked at us to see why the gorilla was looking at us, I was wondering why also. My daddy said to me that the gorilla's instincts told him that we were hunters or that he sensed us as a threat. Of course, we were no threat to him, but I learned a lot about instincts.

We have instincts, but sometimes we have to develop them.

How do you develop your instincts? Always be aware of your surroundings. Look at and observe other people. I heard a police officer say that when he is in a restaurant or other public place, he looks at whoever comes in, and also looks at their hands and waistbands. He watches their mannerisms and how they carry themselves. He said he does it without having to think about it.

Use your hearing. Listen and be aware of any sounds of danger. For example, I have noticed that when I hear a car backfire, I tend to jump and look around, even though I quickly realize it was just a backfire. I've seen others have the same reaction, but sometimes, I see other people who have no reaction at all. Did they hear it, but their minds very quickly processed that it wasn't a gunshot and was only a vehicle backfiring? I don't think so; I think their minds didn't process it at all.

I've seen people walk across the street in front of an oncoming car. It seems that their minds don't process it as dangerous.

Pray that God will help you in developing your instincts. Pray that the Holy Spirit will guide you.

Training

What kind of training would help ensure your survival and the survival of others? There are self-defense courses and martial arts training. There are survival courses. There are first-aid and CPR courses.

We can practice keeping our instincts sharp by watching and observing people. If you get attuned to people's reactions, then you get better at spotting something out of the ordinary.

We can train to keep ourselves in shape. We can train to react quickly and work to become quicker.

We can train ourselves to learn directions by knowing what time of day it is and knowing where the sun should be in the sky. We can learn to tell directions by looking at the moss on the trees or at the denseness of trees on the mountains. We can learn to tell directions by looking at the stars.

We never know when our training could help us to survive or help others. A couple of employees from the refinery where I work attended the concert in Las Vegas that was the scene of a mass shooting in 2017. They were trained in CPR and first aid because they were first responders at the refinery. They were able to help others by using their training.

Alone in Public

My children and I once rode in the car with a female real estate agent who was showing us some homes. When we finished, she wanted to run into a store to pick up something. It was dark as she pulled up to the storefront, and she hesitated before getting out. She said, "You see that man sitting in his car, alone? If I was by myself, I would leave now and go somewhere else, without getting out."

She was aware of her surroundings, and she took certain precautions for her safety. She said she always looked around before getting out of her car. While in stores and before walking out of the stores, she would look around again to make sure no one was following her.

I think every woman should take some kind of self-defense class or survival course; actually, men should too, especially young men.

I did a computer search on *safety*, *survival*, and *self-defense classes*, and I found a lot of classes for women, but there are some available for men. My older children took martial arts training as they were growing up, and I'm getting ready to enroll the younger ones.

Escape Plan

Always plan an escape route. When selecting seats for a movie, concert, or other events or when in a restaurant, consider an escape route when deciding where to sit. If you are seated, look around and make an escape route in your head. Find the exits, including emergency exits. Have alterative escape routes in mind too. I'm not talking about living in fear; it's living aware and prepared.

If I'm sitting in a restaurant or other public place, I am not comfortable unless I'm facing the entrance. If I can get my back to a wall, I'm even more comfortable. I am reminded about a satirical western movie that poked fun of other westerns. There was a scene in a saloon in which everyone was sitting with their backs against the wall. All the walls had people sitting with their backs to the wall, and the rest of the room was wide open and empty. Now, that's a bit extreme. Everyone can't sit with their backs against the wall, but everyone can be aware of the surroundings

Shots Fired Outside

Suppose you are outside, and you hear shots fired. What should you do? First, make yourself the smallest target possible by getting low to the ground. Figure out where the shots came from, and take cover behind something. If you have to run, then do so in a zigzag pattern, and stay low.

Selfless Heroes

As I mentioned, two refinery employees who were trained in first aid helped others after the mass shooting in Las Vegas. I heard about a lot of other heroes that day, such as those who shielded others with their own bodies.

Years ago, my mother and baby sister were in a Magic Mart (a department/discount store) in the Ozarks part of Arkansas when a tornado hit the building and tore off the roof. As the tornado approached, a stranger grabbed my mother and sister. He put my sister on the floor next to some shelves, put my mother on top of my sister, and then covered them with his body. They didn't know who he was and never saw him again after that event, but I am thankful and grateful for him.

Always be ready and willing to help others. Like the employees from the refinery that I mentioned, the more training you have, the more you can help.

Use Common-Sense Safety Rules

When going out and about in your everyday life, use common-sense safety rules. Be alert so you don't get hurt in accidents.

As I've mentioned, always walk with your head up, watching your surroundings, and listen. Don't walk with your head down, reading or poking at an electronic device, such as a phone.

If you're walking or running along a road or highway, use the sidewalk or path, if one is next, so a curb or at least a space is between you and automobile traffic. If there is no walkway, and you have to walk on the roadway, then always walk facing traffic. That means if the automobiles drive on the right like here in the United States, then you walk on the left, facing traffic. The reason is simple: you can watch oncoming traffic as it approaches.

If you are walking with others, walk single file. Recently, I saw a couple of young ladies walking side by side, with their backs to traffic. They were talking while they walked and seemingly were unaware of the passing cars.

There is a small memorial at the edge of the road near our home for a young girl who died after being hit by a car. It happened before I lived there, but I heard that three young girls were walking with their backs to traffic. The driver, another young lady, was looking at her phone as she drove, and she hit the girls, killing one and injuring another.

A friend of mine who used to travel on the side of the road with a motorized wheelchair was hit and killed while traveling home from church. He was killed by a drunk driver. If you drink, don't drive.

If you are on a bicycle, the law requires you to travel on the same side of the road that cars travel. This is because a bicycle is faster than walking, and if you meet a car on the road and you are facing the car, neither of you would have time to react. If you are riding with traffic, then then the car has more time to react and adjust, if need be.

If you are driving, keep your eyes on the road. Don't text, and don't watch a movie. Once, I was in traffic on the freeway, and I noticed the man driving in front of me was watching a movie. His DVD player was in the middle of his dashboard, and he watched the screen when stopped in traffic and glanced at it when traffic was moving.

Keep a knife with you that's capable of cutting a seat belt. My daddy told me that he always carries a sharp knife for this reason. He was a policeman for twenty years and had to cut seat belts on occasion to get someone out of a wrecked car. A pocket knife will do the job.

Keep a lighter in your pocket as well. I carry a lighter because once, when I was a youngster, my daddy, grandfather, uncle, and I were deer hunting and staying in the woods for a few days. It was a very remote area; we had to take a boat to get there. It got so cold that year. I was sitting up on a deer stand, shaking, and realized that it was too cold for the deer to be out; they would be huddled up by a fire somewhere to keep warm. I thought, *That is what I need to do. I need to build a fire and warm up.* I climbed down from the stand and gathered up a little wood and some dried grass.

My grandfather used to say that some men build great big fires and sit far away to keep warm, and we build small fires and sit close to keep warm. So my fire was going to be a little fire, just big enough for me. I cleared the debris from around the fire area, which had dried wood on the bottom and dried grass on top. I was already proud of the fire that was going to warm me. Then I realized that I didn't have any way to start it. I reached into every pocket, as if a lighter or matches would appear there. I decided to rub two sticks together to start a fire—at least, that's what I tried to do. I got a couple of sticks and rubbed them together, but I wasn't able to start the fire. Still, the rubbing action kept me warm.

As I was sitting next to my little campfire with no fire, my daddy walked up. I asked him if he had a lighter or matches, but he said we were leaving because it was too cold. We went back to our camp, where my grandfather and uncle already had started to pack up.

When we got back home, my grandmother asked about two local men who were hunting in the same general area that we were. We found out later that they didn't make it out alive, unfortunately, they froze to death.

- Always be aware of your surroundings, and be watchful.
- In a shooting situation, take cover, and make yourself as small a target as possible.
- Help others in any way you can.
- Be prepared.

CHAPTER 5
PROTECTING YOURSELF AT HOME

How do you protect yourself and your children at home?

Lock Your Doors

When I was growing up in rural Arkansas, we didn't lock our doors—but that was a different time. Nowadays, I lock my doors.

Be careful who you open your doors to. I have heard of people wearing utility company uniforms to gain access to homes and then rob them. I have heard of a harmless-looking woman knocking on the door, and when the door is opened, a man or men, who had been out of sight, force their way inside. Don't open the door to strangers. Don't let workmen into your home unless you called them to come. If workers show up unannounced, tell them their office will have to make an appointment. Then, when they call to make an appointment, call them back on a verified number to confirm the appointment.

What if someone comes to your door, needing help? Aren't we supposed to help anyone who asks? Well, we aren't supposed to put ourselves in danger. Most people have cell phones. If someone comes to your door needing help, and that person doesn't have a cell phone, keep the door locked, keep yourself safe, and call the police, and let that person know you have called the police for help for them.

Instruct your children and the adults in your home not to open the door to strangers. In the United States, you don't even have to let police in your home unless they have a warrant. There have been instances where people have dressed as police to gain access to a home in order to rob the place.

Firearms in the Home

I saw a comic picture once of two homes, side by side. A sign in front of one of the homes read, "Dear robbers, my neighbor doesn't believe in owning guns, but I do."

We have firearms in our home. I have been around firearms all my life. I was a grown man when I found out that not everybody has firearms. It's a personal choice to own guns.

Of course, not every household should have firearms. Perhaps someone in the home is a mean drunk, or maybe someone in the house is mentally or emotionally unstable. There may be other reasons why a firearm in the home isn't a good choice.

If you do own firearms, however, make sure they are secure from children, and make sure you and your family are trained in the proper and safe use of them.

As I said, I was raised around firearms. When I was five years old or maybe younger, we children were eating dinner when my daddy came in the house with a rifle—he'd been hunting or doing target practice. He leaned the rifle against the wall just a few feet from us while he washed his hands. We just knew we weren't supposed to touch it because if we did, it could be deadly. Had it been a poisonous snake, we would have been danger with it that close, and we wouldn't have been at ease, but the rifle was an inanimate object. As long as the rifle just sat there, we were fine.

Nowadays, I don't let my firearms within my children's reach, but I do let them know they must not touch firearms unless I'm giving them instructions.

Once when my young children and I were visiting my parents, we stayed in a guest room that my younger sister had stayed in fairly recently. Later, my children came to me and said they had found a gun in the dresser drawer. I immediately went to look, but it turned out to be a lighter that looked like a pistol. I explained what it was and then commended them for doing what I had taught them—not touching it and letting me know. I was happy that they had done what I had taught them, and I thought, *What if they hadn't been taught, and it had been a real gun?* Teach your children what to do if they see firearms—don't touch, and get an adult.

Regarding owning a gun, I offer the following analogy: Suppose there is a place where people don't have guns. A mob with machetes and clubs overtakes a home. They don't know how many people are in the home, and they don't know the strength of the people inside, but they know if the mob is large enough, they will overpower the people in the home.

If, however, it's a place where people have guns, the mob doesn't know if the people inside have guns or the potential firepower of the people inside. I heard of a gun battle where the chief of police in another country was able to withstand a people attacking his home from the outside, although he was far outnumbered.

Other Dangers in the Home

Make sure that you are protected against accidents, such as fire. If you don't have safety guidelines, go to your local fire department and ask them for safety guidelines. Install smoke detectors in each room. Make sure fire extinguishers are easily accessible, with at least one on each floor. Install a carbon monoxide detector or alarm, placed near the kitchen and heaters, stoves, or fireplaces. If there are multiple floors in the home have rope ladders or some means of escape on the upper floors.

Christmas Trees

In many parts of the world, the yearly tradition is to bring in an evergreen tree and decorate it with lights and ornaments. If these trees dry out, they are very combustible. I recall when I was young some relatives were killed in a fire caused by Christmas tree lights. Nowadays, there are different kinds of bulbs that are not as hazardous, but still, a dry evergreen tree in the home is very flammable.

Emergency Supplies

Make sure you have one or more first-aid kits. Have one in each vehicle as well. You can buy first-aid kits already assembled, or assemble one yourself.

Store enough water to last at the minimum of three days. Figure at least three gallons for each person in the household. If you have room then store more. Also, purchase a water purifier and familiarize yourself on how to use it.

For a little more water storage, consider not placing cleaning chemicals in the tank of a toilet. The tanks are isolated from the toilet bowls and are not contaminated.

Make sure you have nonperishable food to last at least three days. Three weeks is better, three months is even better.

Some companies specialize in nonperishable food for emergencies. Military MREs ("meals ready to eat") are good to have, if you can get them. Canned goods, honey, and other foods that last a long time without being refrigerated are good to store.

Make sure you have flashlights, lanterns, and/or candles. If you want, consider having a generator as backup if the power goes out.

Have easy-to-transport, emergency, get-out-of-here kits. I've heard them called *bug-out bags*. You can buy them premade, or you can assemble them yourself. The idea is to use the bags if you suddenly have to leave your home; you can grab the bags, which contain necessary supplies, and go. Consider having small bug-out bags in each vehicle.

Don't forget your pets. I breed German shepherds, so I store extra bags of dog food. I consider this: if we run out of food, then dog food is better than starving, and if everything runs out, look out dogs. I spoke to a man whose brother has horses, and his brother told him that the horses are part of his emergency food plan. Of course, I wouldn't eat dog food or the dogs or horses until all the food, including emergency supply of food, was depleted.

Make sure you have some type of home protection. If you can afford it, install an alarm system. If you have a fenced yard, make sure you can secure it. Make sure your window and door locks work.

Here in the United States, I recommend putting up a flag. I've heard it said that robbers pass by the homes that fly the American flag because they think the home is more likely to be armed.

Have an emergency plan in case of attackers. If you have firearms, make sure you are well trained, and of course, make sure your firearms are not accessible to young children.

If you can, have an escape room in the house—a room that you can run into and lock. Some safe rooms actually are bulletproof and fireproof survival shelters or panic rooms that can be installed in a home, but even if you just install a solid door to a room with a secure lock, it's better than the average hollow interior door.

Make sure your vehicles stay fueled up and ready to go. Store extra fuel somewhere safe.

If you have firearms in your home, they must be in a safe place, out of reach of children. Don't tell people outside your home the location of your guns and ammunition. Store at least a few boxes of ammunition. Train and practice using firearms safely.

- Lock your doors.
- Have a safety and security plan.
- Store extra water and food.
- Keep vehicles ready to go.
- Have a safe and secured room in the home.
- If you have firearms in the home, keep them inaccessible to children.
- Keep extra ammunition.

CHAPTER 6
PROTECTING OUR MOST INNOCENT

I COULDN'T WRITE this book about protecting our lives without mentioning the most innocent lives that don't have any rights and are not even regarded as human by some in our society.

Some years ago, my wife was carrying in her womb our daughter, Rachel Ida Lee. Our baby was named after my wife's grandmother, Rachel, and my grandmother, whose middle name was Ida Lee. We had gotten to know Rachel by seeing her in ultrasounds and hearing her heartbeat. As I did for all my children, I sang and read and talked to her when she was in the womb.

But then one day, when my wife was about seven months pregnant, she told me that the baby hadn't been moving much. I took my wife to the hospital, where a nurse admitted her. The nurse couldn't hear our baby's heartbeat. A doctor came in, but she too could not hear the baby's heartbeat. The doctor told us that our baby had died in the womb.

Later, she explained that our baby would get a birth certificate and death certificate and that my wife would have induced labor. I was told to make burial arrangements.

Sometime later, it occurred to me that our baby who had died in the womb had more rights and was regarded higher than our society regards a living baby in the womb. In our society, a living baby in the womb can be regarded only as a piece of flesh, like an unwanted tumor, and sucked out in pieces and disposed of. Our baby, Rachel Ida Lee Pruett, who died in the womb, was officially given a name, and it was written on a paper, recognizing her; there is a marker in a cemetery where her remains are buried, with her name and her birth date and death date. My wife and I know she isn't there; she is in heaven, where we want to go someday.

In our society, if it something is said often enough and loud enough, it often is accepted as a fact, whether or not it is true. We are told that a baby in the womb isn't a person or isn't human. Every one of us has been in the womb. Every human that ever lived, other than Adam, Eve, and Melchizedek, has been a baby in the womb.

We see in the scriptures that while in the womb, God knows us (Psalm 139:13–16; Jeremiah 1:5).

When I was in the womb, I was already me. Sure, I was developing, but so is a child. When I was a baby, I developed into a child, then I developed into a teenager, and then I developed into an adult. If I had died in the womb or died as a child or a teenager then I wouldn't be here as a grown man today. That is simple logic, yet some people say that a baby in the womb isn't a baby, or isn't human.

Today's society teaches that if one has the desire to engage in the act of reproduction, then just do what you desire, and if a baby is conceived, just ignore that it's a baby and rip it out.

A president of the United States asked, if his daughter had sex and got pregnant, should she be punished by having a baby? So it is accepted in our society that a man and a woman engage in the act of reproduction, and then when a baby is produced, it is a punishment, and it is okay to kill that baby.

There are abortion-pushers who don't want it said that if you don't want a baby, then don't have sex, and if you do have sex, then use contraception. There was a woman who said that she wished she had had an abortion so she could be like her mother and aunt. Really? She wished she had conceived a child, just to have the child torn from her womb?

Recently, a state governor was recorded as condoning killing babies after birth if they have survived an attempted abortion. As a result, a bill was introduced in the United States Congress that requires lifesaving measures for a baby who survives an attempted abortion, but the bill was voted down. Let me say that again: the bill that would require lifesaving medical attention for a baby that survived an abortion was rejected.

Nowadays, some politicians don't even pretend that that they believe a baby in the womb isn't a baby. One recently said, "Kill a baby that isn't wanted now, or kill it later," claiming that if babies aren't wanted, they will grow up to commit crimes that will land them in the electric chair. What nonsense!

It's not just politicians; a lot of people have such hard hearts that they believe it's okay to kill a baby. They like to say, "Let it be the mother's choice."

Let it be the mother's choice before a child is conceived. Let it also be the man's choice not to get a woman pregnant.

With the logic of its being the mother's choice, where does it end? Will they make it okay that the mother has the option to kill their child as long as he/she lives?

We live in an evil society.

What can we do?

I won't vote for anyone who says it's okay to kill babies, in the womb or not.

Today's society condones killing babies in the womb by screaming that it's the woman's body, and a woman has the right to do what she wants to do with her own body. But a baby in the womb is not the woman's body. A baby in the womb is an individual body, forming in and dependent on the mother's body. That's just how it works, but it isn't the mother's body.

For example, if a baby in the womb was the mother's body, then if the baby's heartbeat stopped, the mother would die. But, the mother doesn't die; because it's not her heartbeat, it's not her body, a body can't live without its heartbeat; the baby dies.

Let's teach our sons and daughters not to have sex before marriage, but it they do and don't want a pregnancy, then use contraception. Let's teach our children to be responsible for their actions.

If contraception doesn't work, then there are many good people who would be happy to adopt a child.

- Be smart and responsible.
- If you don't want a pregnancy, use contraception.
- If contraception doesn't work, consider adoption if you are unable or don't want to raise the child.
- We all had our start in the womb.

CHAPTER 7
STOP SUICIDES

I HEAR ABOUT so many suicides these days. Any suicide is senseless and tragic, and I feel sad any time I here of one, but more so when I hear of a child, veteran, or a member of the military.

Giving Power to Bullies

Self-Confidence

I have heard about the senseless deaths of children, whereas they heard or read that someone said cruel things about them, and so they killed themselves. It is sad that these young people didn't know the value of their own lives and that they put so much credence into what someone else said.

I heard the popular saying when I was young: *Sticks and stones may break my bones, but words may never hurt me.*

My wife told me in her country, Ghana, she heard something like this: "If someone tells you that you are a goat, does that make you a goat? You know you are not a goat, so if someone tells you that you are a goat, it should be meaningless gibber to you."

Children need to be built up and encouraged to be strong. They need to know that they are created in God's image and that they are special.

Children also need to be taught not to let words have power over them. Growing up my uncle picked on me. Sometimes, such as when we went hunting or fishing, my uncle, my grandfather, and my daddy picked on me. My uncle also picked on my cousins. He did it because he loved us and was teaching us not to be weak and whiny. If we'd whine or cry about it, it would only get worse. It was to make us strong.

By the time I went to school, when someone tried to pick on me by saying something mean, I would think, *Is this intended to upset me? Is that all you got?*

When my oldest daughter was a child, she came home from school one day and said some girls were trying to bully her.

I asked, "Did they hit you or push you? Pop them in the nose if they did."

She said, "No, they only were saying mean things."

I said, "Words don't hurt you. It's your own feelings that hurt you if you give the words power to trigger your feelings."

I then had a class with her and my son. I told her to say something mean to me.

She said, "You have a big nose."

I said, "Oh, thank you for noticing. Did you think that up by yourself? That was creative."

Then she called me "baldy."

I said, "Thank you for noticing. I cut my hair myself."

Or I'd tell her to say something mean, and I'd just be quiet and walk off, or I'd swat the air with my hand like I was swatting a fly and say, "Oh, I hear this fly that is just trying to bug me," and then I'd walk away.

Then I told my daughter, "Let me say something to you."

When I did, she replied with something like I had taught her, shrugged it off, and walked away. Then she and my son practiced on each other.

When my children were in martial arts class, the teacher would ask the class, "Do you think you are somebody special?"

All the children would answer, "I am someone special!"

We have to teach our children to be self-confident and strong. We have to teach them that someone else's words do not have power over them. We have to teach them that they are important. We have to teach our children that their lives are precious.

Teach your children that they are special.

Military

I love and respect our military members and our veterans; we owe so much to them. These men and women step up to protect us and our freedoms. They go through so much, in example, being away from their loved ones; and many are exposed to so much more horror. Some of our military members come back with post-traumatic stress disorder. I read that the number of military members and veterans who kill themselves is rising; even one is too many.

What can we do? If you are a family member or friend or know veterans or military members, let them know how much you appreciate their service to our country. With all respect to them, ask how they are doing. I say "with respect" because it can't be assumed that military personnel and veterans have problems just because of their military service. When you ask, be sincere, caring, and respectful. And again, thank them for their service. Let them know you sincerely care about them and are thankful for them.

Whether or not you have served or are serving, if you have thoughts of harming yourself, know that your life is precious. Call a suicide prevention hotline, reach out, and get professional help.

If you or anyone you know has thoughts about suicide, call a helpline, or reach out and get help. Be strong, and keep your head up.

- Your life is precious. Every person's life is precious.
- Nothing is made better by ending your life.

- Overcome your life challenges and obstacles; stay strong.
- If you or anyone you know has considered suicide, call a helpline, talk to a preacher or someone, reach out, and get help.

CHAPTER 8
POLICE

I LOVE AND appreciate the police. My daddy was a police officer for twenty years. I was accepted to the Los Angeles County Sheriff's Department but was disqualified when I was being processed in because I'm deaf in one ear. I appreciate the job that police do in keeping us safe.

All over the world, the system in place for law and order is law enforcement officers in some form—police department, sheriff's department, state troopers, constables, marshals, or FBI. Thousands or maybe millions of officers do their jobs every day without incident. It's a protect-and-serve law-and-order system.

Protect-and-Serve Law and Order

My daddy saved people's lives; he handled various situations in a positive way, and had he handled the situations differently, there could have been loss of life. Once, my daddy and other officers answered a call at a local hotel—a man was standing in the middle of the parking lot in the rain, wearing only his underwear, looking up at the sky and praying and hollering. After assessing the situation, my daddy walked out into the rain and stood next to the man. He looked up at the sky with his hands out, like the man, and began praying.

The man stopped and looked at my daddy. "What are you doing?" the man asked him.

"What are *you* doing?" my daddy asked the man.

The man answered, "God told me to go outside and pray."

My daddy said, "God told me that you have done well, and you can stop and go back to your room."

The man quietly went back to his room.

On another occasion, a family reported that an elderly member of their family was missing. My daddy drove around, looking for the elderly man. When he found the man walking by the highway, my daddy stopped to talk to the man, but the man wouldn't stop walking.

The man told my daddy, "God told me to walk east, so I am going to walk east."

My daddy said, "What will you do when you come to the river?"

The man repeated, "God told me to walk east, and I am going to walk east."

My daddy said, "God told me to tell you that you have done well, and you can stop walking east now."

The man then agreed to get in the car with my daddy.

Years later, I was talking to a friend who told me about an uncle who had insisted that God told him to walk east. When his uncle came to the river, he kept walking and drowned.

I believe that most police officers are like my daddy and genuinely care about people; they want to protect and serve. In recent tragic events, however, unarmed people have been killed by police; in some situations, the people were armed for protection, but perhaps it could have been handled differently, without the loss of life.

When Stopped by Police

If you are stopped by the police, remember they don't know anything about you. If you are stopped by police while driving a car, keep your hands on the steering wheel. Do not have anything in your hands. Keep your hands on each side of the steering wheel.

If the police approach you when you are on foot, make sure your hands are empty, and if you're carrying anything, drop it. Hold your hands where they are clearly visible.

I once did my daily mile walk at night on the side of the road near my house, and I had a large flashlight in my hand. I heard a vehicle behind me and noticed its headlights brighten. I immediately dropped the flashlight to the ground and raised my hands. It was police, and I told them that I was doing my walk. They explained that they'd had a call indicating that someone was walking around with a gun. If I had spun around with the flashlight in my hand, they might have mistaken it for a gun.

If you're stopped, whether in your car or on foot, be respectful; answer with a *sir* or *ma'am*. Be polite and speak clearly, and say, "Good morning [or *good afternoon*], Officer." This will show you are not a threat. Introduce yourself, and if the officer responds by telling you his or her name, address him or her by name and title (such as, *Officer Jones*) from then on. If they haven't told you, ask them what organization they represent. Whatever you say, keep your tone calm and clear. Don't sound hostile or angry.

If you think you are being picked on or have been stopped unjustly, that is not the time to argue. It is the time to cooperate, and if you believe there was any injustice, place a complaint later by going to the police station or contacting a local elected official.

Do not get excitable. Do not be argumentative. Do not act in a hostile manner. Do not raise your voice. Do not make sudden moves or reach into your pockets.

Keep your hands visible. Do not reach for anything, unless instructed to do so. If asked to show your driver's license or insurance card and registration, announce what you are doing, such as, "Officer, I am retrieving my driver's license." Then move slow and smooth.

As I said, if you are stopped while walking and have something in your hands, drop it. If it's something of value or fragile, and it doesn't look threatening, hold it up with your fingertips, hold your hands up, and tell them what you are holding. (As for me, I would just drop it.)

Instruct your children on what to do if stopped by police. I was teaching my son how to shoot a BB gun in our backyard. The first thing I told him was this: "If you see the police coming around the corner of the house, drop the BB gun immediately, and hold your hands in the air. Suppose a neighbor has called the police, reporting that someone is shooting. The police wouldn't know that we just had a BB gun. They would see a gun and react accordingly—in seconds."

Police Training

Every day, law enforcement officers place themselves in dangerous situations, and most go through extensive training to ensure that they and the public stay safe. They have to train continuously.

When my daddy was a police officer, he was also the chief training officer in his small city department. He told the officers that if someone were to draw a gun on them, they should stop the individual by firing three rounds into the chest area. Then, if the person continued being a threat, they should fire three more rounds.

I've heard on the news that people are shot so many times by police that the officers involved must be shooting until their firearms are empty.

Inquire with your local law enforcement as to the training of their officers. Express your concern that the officers should have continuous, extensive training on when and when not to use deadly force.

Make sure you educate yourself as to what is possible and reasonable. For example, don't think that officers should be trained to shoot someone in the leg. Deadly force should be used only when the officer's life or an individual's life is immediately at risk; or if the perpetrator will get away, and it's highly probable that he will be a threat to someone's life. The purpose of deadly force is to stop an immediate threat to life. Shooting someone in the leg does not always stop the person who is the immediate threat.

- If stopped by police, remain calm.
- Do not make sudden moves.
- Do not reach for anything unless requested to do so.

CHAPTER 9
THE BIBLE AND THE BOOK OF REVELATION

I AM A follower of Jesus Christ, and I encourage everyone to read the Holy Bible and obey the gospel. The Bible is full of God's love to us. In the Bible, there is history and prophecy.

In Matthew 16:26, Jesus Christ asked, "For what will it profit a man if he gains the whole world and forfeits his soul?" I wrote about protecting our lives, but our souls are more important.

Read the Bible daily; there are different ways to do this. You could read straight through, like any other book. You could start with Genesis, and read a few verses or chapters every day. Read all the way through.

I recommend, however, starting with the book of

Matthew. Gospels means *good news*, so read the good news. Read the Acts of the Apostles, read through the New Testament, and then read the Old Testament.

You could read the Bible by subject matter; for example, if you want to learn about baptism. Use a concordance to look up every time the word *baptism* is in the Bible.

Suppose you want to study Jesus's parables. Run an internet search on "Jesus's parables in the Bible," and then look them up and study them.

Another way to read the Bible is to open it to a random page, point to a passage, and then read; or just open and read wherever your eyes fall. When I open the Bible and read randomly, whatever I'm reading often is pertinent to something I'm going through at the time.

Do research on the different Bible translations. I've read the King James Version, the New King James Version, the English Standard Version, and the New International Version.

In the 1600s, King James I of England commissioned about forty-seven scholars to translate the Bible into English, which is why it's called the King James Version. The King James Version is written in old

English that was spoken in the seventeenth century. The New King James Version, the English Standard Version, and the New International Version are written in the modern English.

As I understand it, the King James Version, the New King James Version, and the English Standard Version translate word for word, as much as possible.

When I am teaching others, I prefer to use the New King James Version and the English Standard Version because those translations are written in the English we use today. For example, instead of using *thee* and *thou*, as in the 1600s, the translation uses the modern *you*.

The Revelation of Jesus Christ

The book of Revelation is the revelation of Jesus Christ. The book of Revelation contains end-times prophecies. I've seen preachers and teachers skip Revelation when they study and teach the books of the Bible. I read Revelation as a child in the '70s, and I've read it as an adult. I want to point out the differences in my thought processes from when I read it as a child in rural Arkansas and when I read it as an adult.

> Then I saw another beast rising out of
> the earth. It had two horns like a lamb
> and it spoke like a dragon. It exercises
> all the authority of the first beast in its
> presence, and makes the earth and its
> inhabitants worship the first beast, whose
> mortal wound was healed. It performs
> great signs, even making fire come down
> from heaven to earth in front of people,
> and by the signs that it is allowed to work
> in the presence of the beast it deceives
> those who dwell on earth, telling them
> to make an image for the beast that was
> wounded by the sword and yet lived.
> (Revelation 13:11–14 ESV)

Whatever this beast is, it will convince and deceive
the world—all except those sealed by God. If you take
the mark of the beast, it won't turn out well for you
in the end, as you will see as you continue reading.
Teach your future generations.

> And it was allowed to give breath to the
> image of the beast, so that the image of
> the beast might even speak and might

cause those who would not worship the image of the beast to be slain. Also it causes all, both small and great, both rich and poor, both free and slave, to be marked on the right hand or the forehead, so that no one can buy or sell unless he has the mark, that is, the name of the beast or the number of its name. This calls for wisdom: let the one who has understanding calculate the number of the beast, for it is the number of a man, and his number is 666. (Revelations 13:15–18 (ESV)

When I first read this as a child, I thought, *We will just go into the woods and hunt, gather, and grow food.* Today when I read it, I think, *These days, who knows how to hunt and grow food? Many people these days don't even know how to cook.*

How can we survive if we are totally dependent on the government and others? Learn to survive. If you know how to hunt, gather, and grow food, teach it to your children and other young people. If you don't know how to hunt, gather, and grow food, then learn.

Learn how to hunt, gather, and grow food. Learn to defend yourself, and teach your children how to defend themselves.

Stay faithful and stay steadfast, and if you are alive when the end times come, *do not* take the mark of the beast, and teach the Word to our future generations.

We have freedom of religion in the United States. We are free to read, study, and teach the Bible. Yet many people, even believers, don't read the Bible.

In some countries, reading the Bible is illegal, yet the people still read, study, and teach it.

Don't take our freedom of religion for granted.

As I've said, I've read the book of Revelation of Jesus Christ. I encourage everyone to read it. Read the Bible, including Revelation.

The Book of Revelation contains prophesy to those who read it.

> Blessed *is* he who reads and those who hear the words of this prophecy, and keep those things which are written in it; for the time *is* near. (Revelation 1:3 NKJV)

- Read and Study the Bible.
- Obey the gospel.

- Read and study the book of Revelation of Jesus Christ.
- Stay steadfast in the Word.

Peace, and God bless you.

ABOUT THE AUTHOR

DARRIN LEE PRUETT was born and raised in Arkansas, at a time when everyone looked out for each other and helped each other. He grew up in the Mississippi River Delta, in Lee County, as well as in the Ozarks in Izzard County, Arkansas.

He graduated from high school a year early and joined the United States Marine Corps at age seventeen. He served active duty in the marines for a four-year enlistment.

He is blessed to be husband to a beautiful queen from Ghana and father to five children, as well as having a son-in-law, daughter-in-law, and two grandchildren. He sees his family as his God-given responsibility and his most valuable treasure.

He is a believer and follower of the Lord God Almighty and His Son, our Lord and Savior Jesus Christ.

He considers himself a simple man and thinks in simple terms. The suggestions and ideas he puts forth in this book also are simple, although some people may not see them as simple.

Printed in the United States
By Bookmasters